What We Have in Common

A Brim Coloring Book

Written by Jane Landey
Edited by David Austin
Copyright©2017

Drawings by David Austin and Jane Austin
Published by CreateSpace: An Amazon Company.
Printed in U.S.A.

Introduction
What We Have in Common.

Brim Coloring Books enable children to color as they read along!

They display the similarities of related animals. In this series the worm and the snake are compared. The facts enable children to appreciate common values. Thus, imbibing in them interest towards animals which could make them appreciate what they have in common with one another.

The Worm

And

The Snake

The worm and the snake have things in common. They wriggle and love to crawl in the soil.

The worm and the snake meet along a path.

I am a worm.

I am a snake.

I can wriggle.

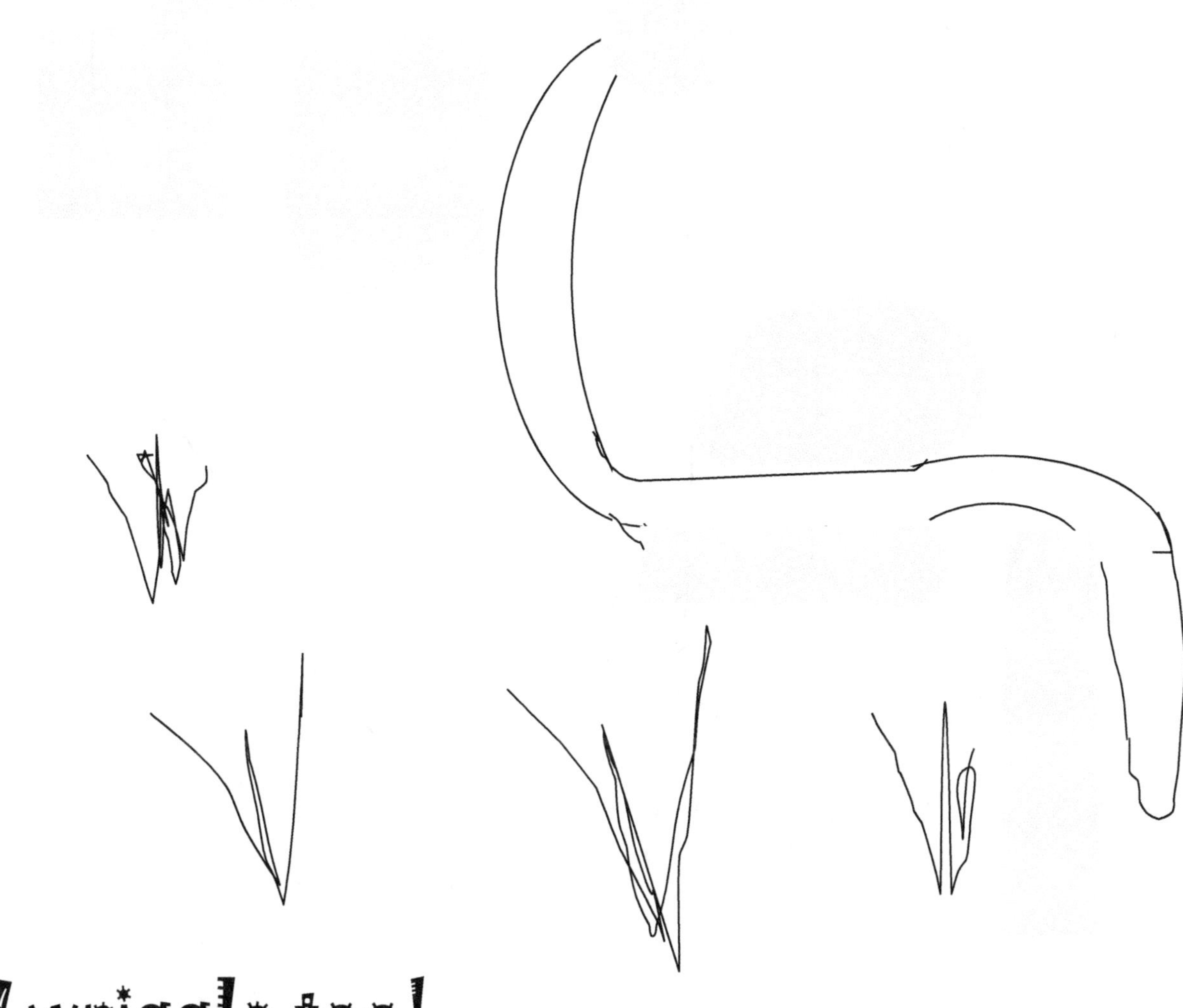

I wriggle too!

I hide in the soil.

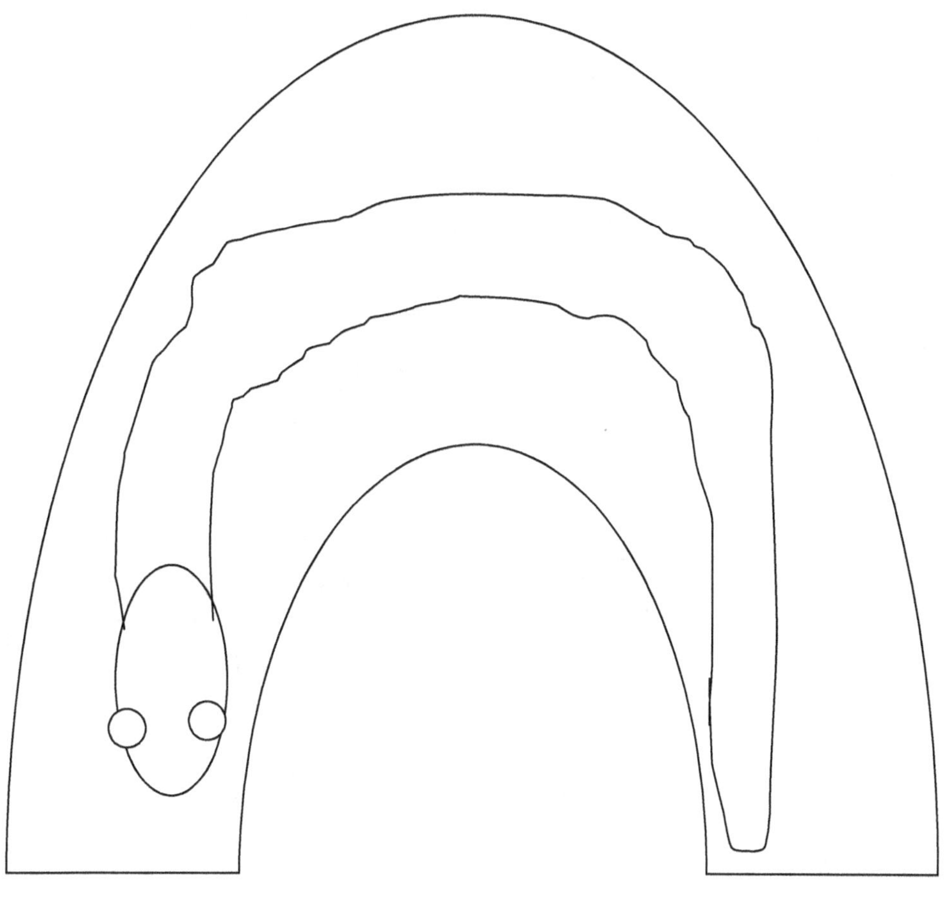

I hide in a hole.

I can play on a branch.

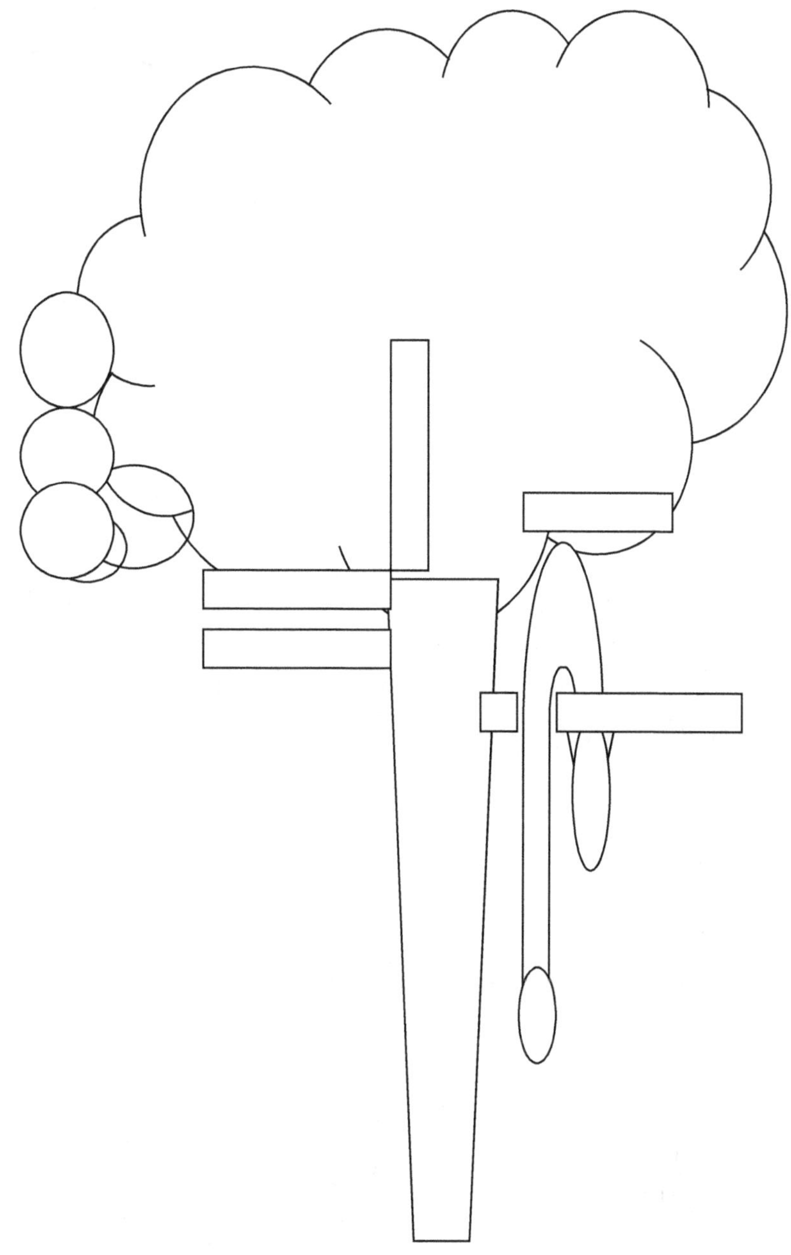

So can I!

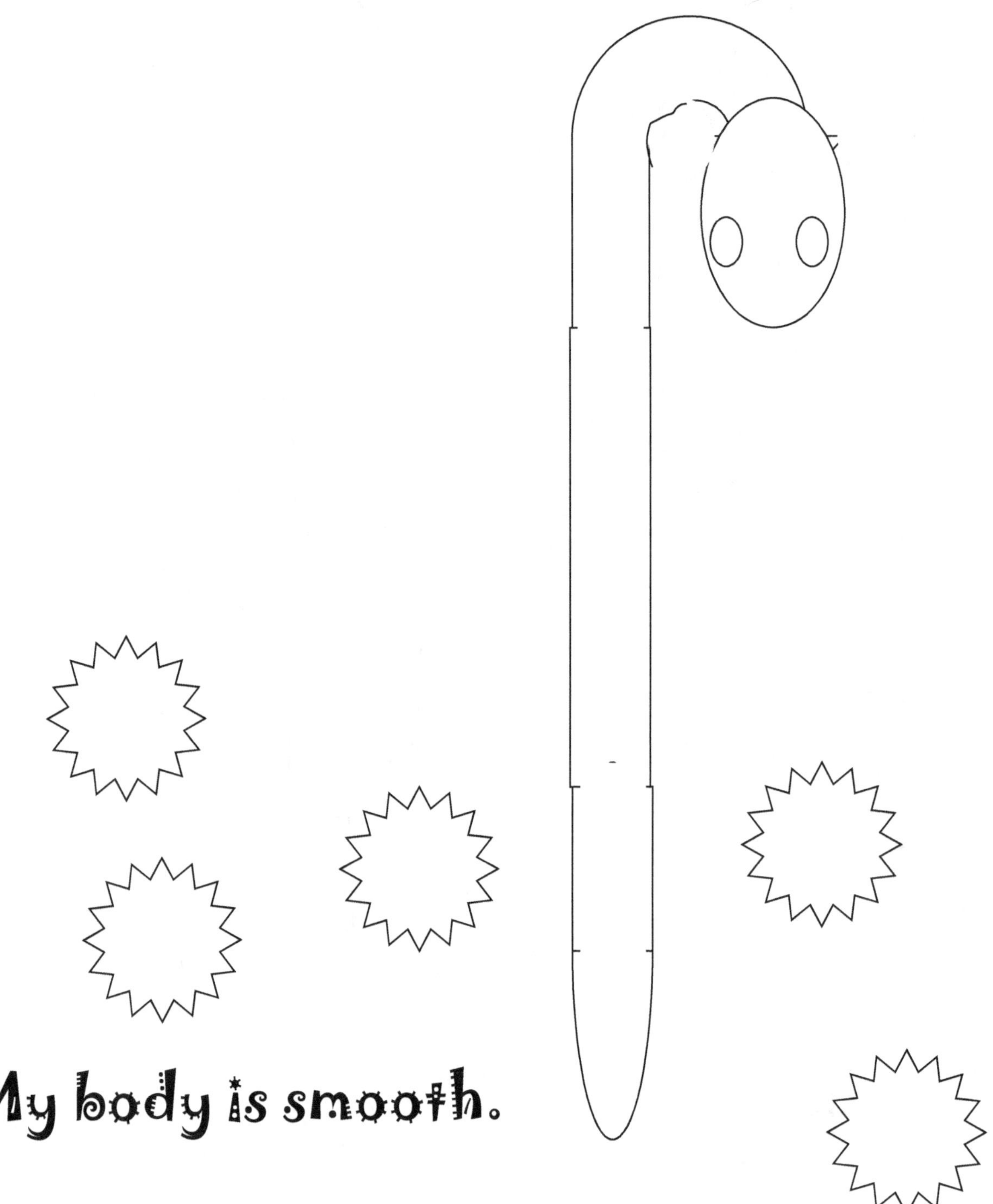

My body is smooth.

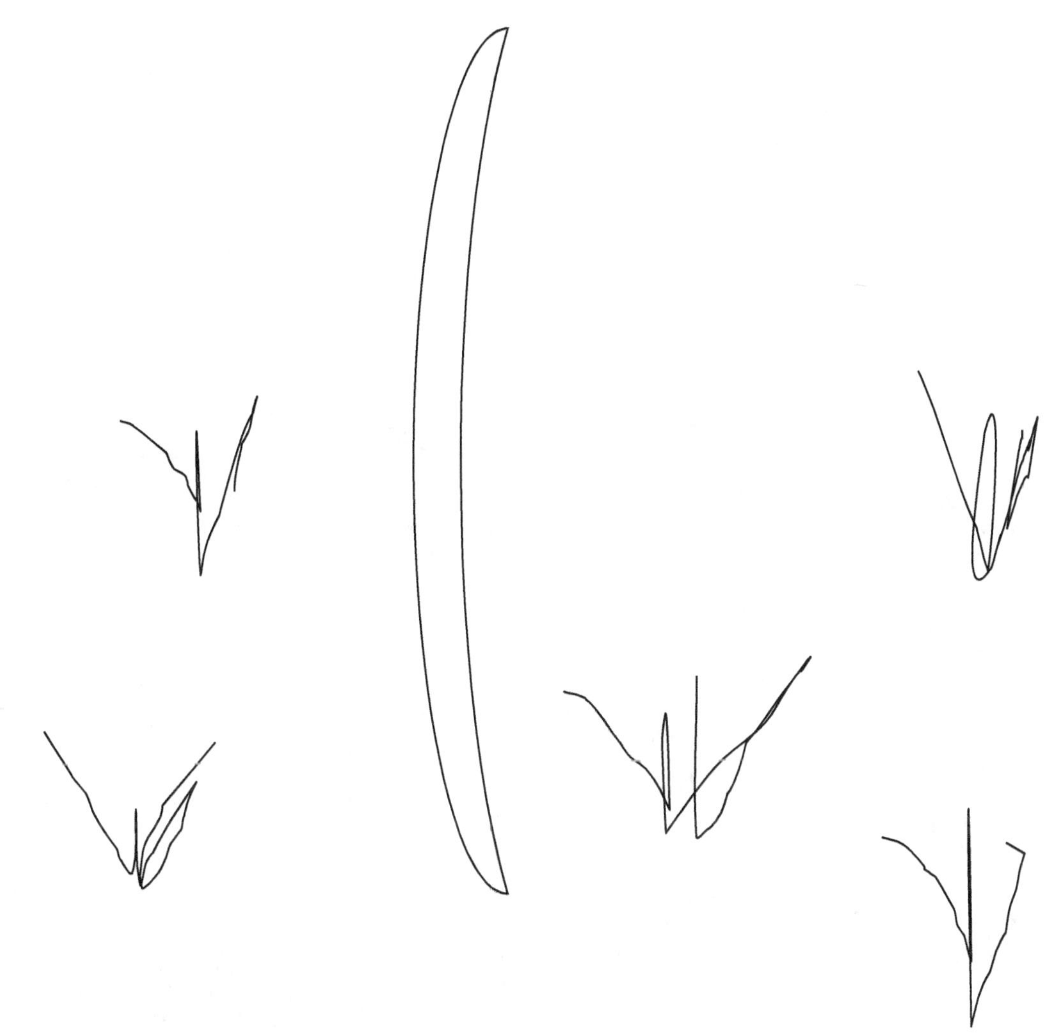

My body is smooth too!

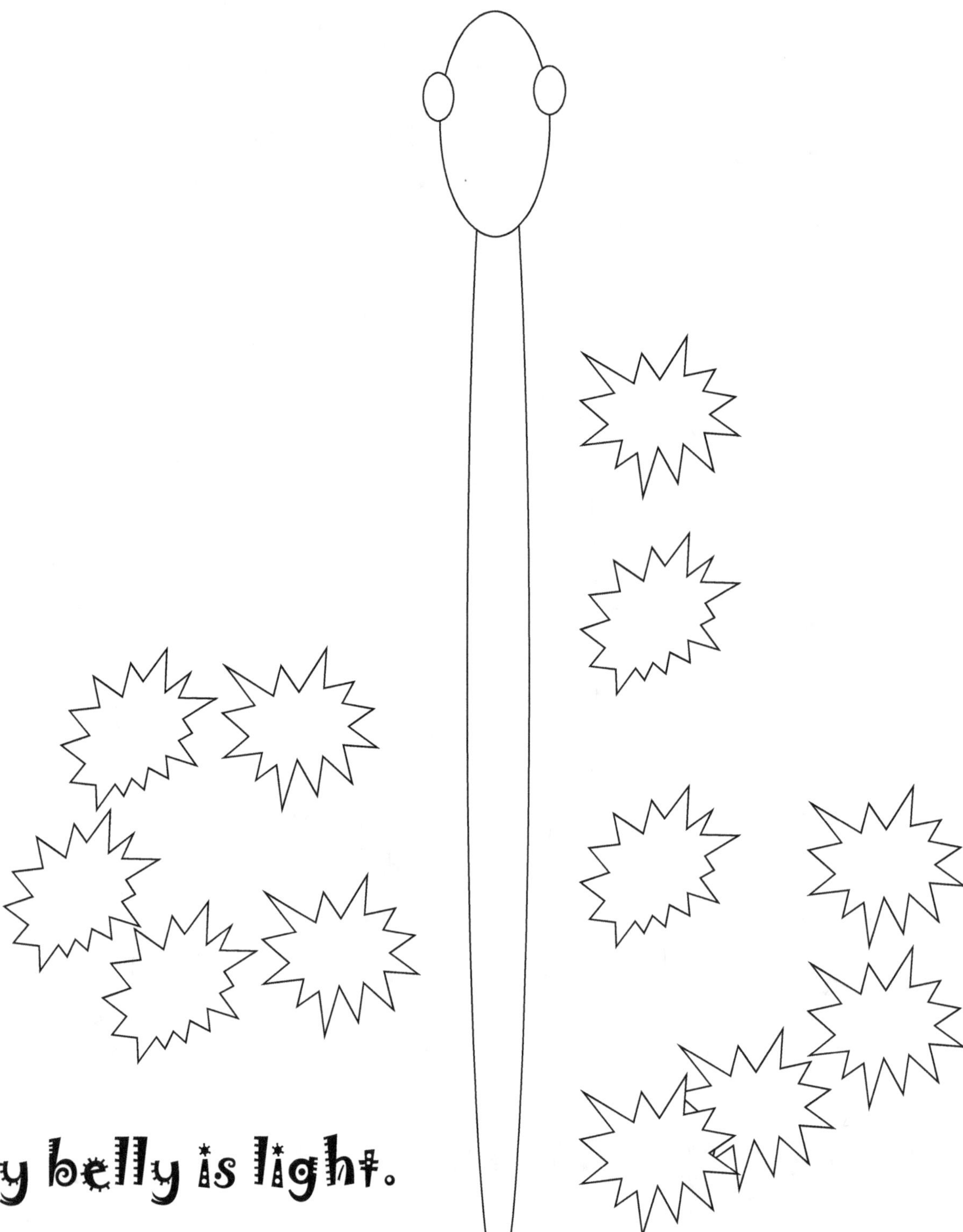

My belly is light.

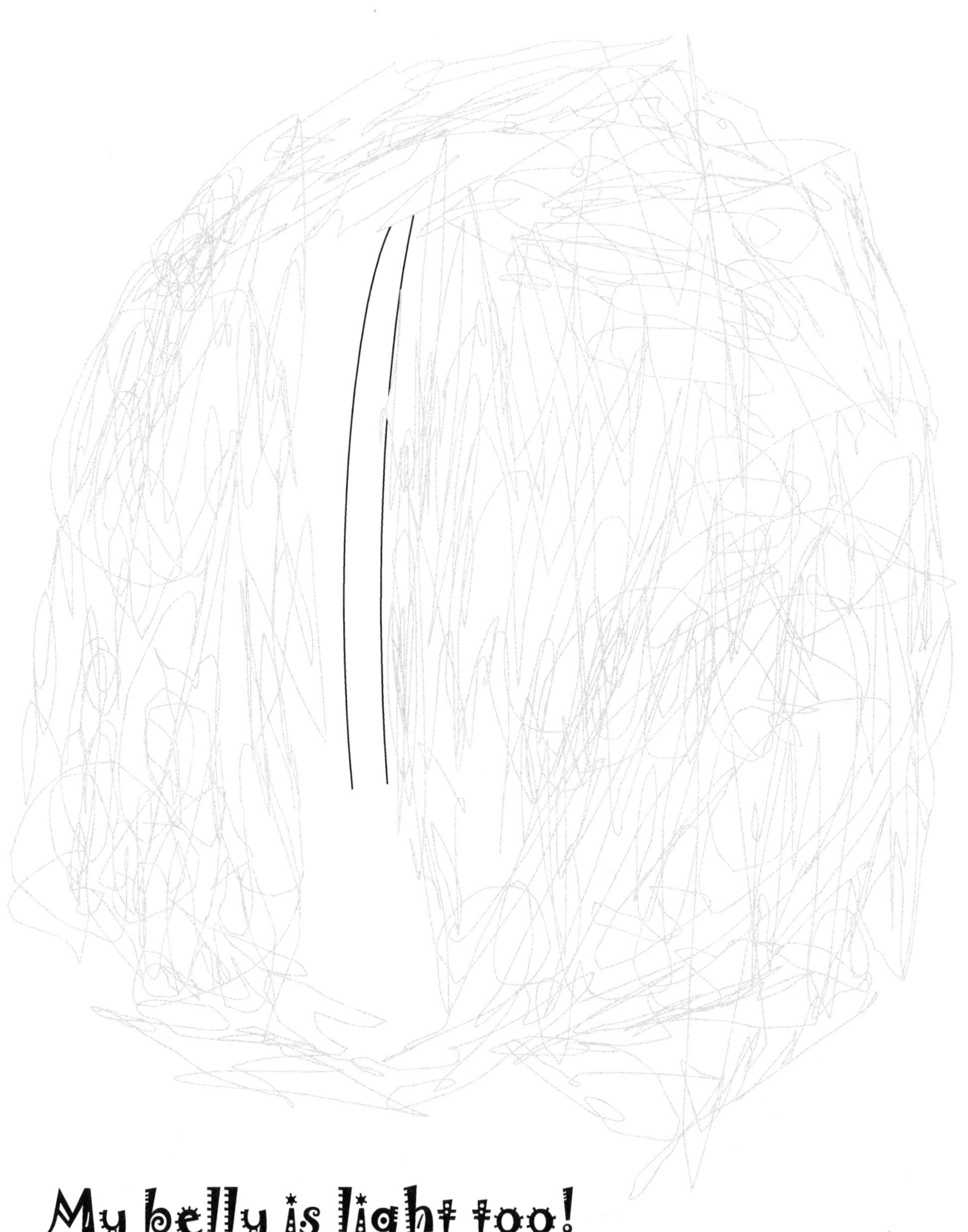

My belly is light too!

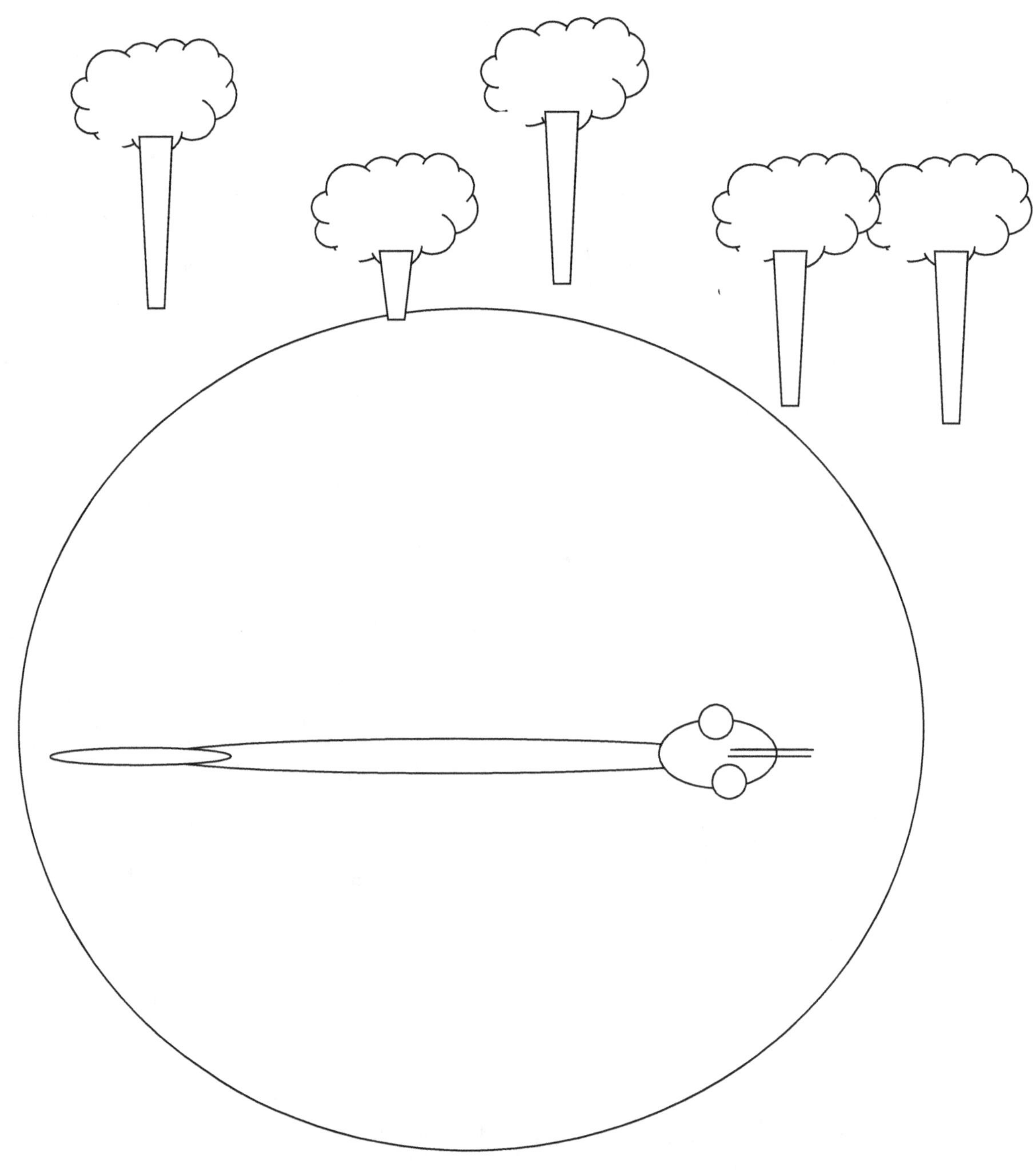

I drink water.

I drink water too!

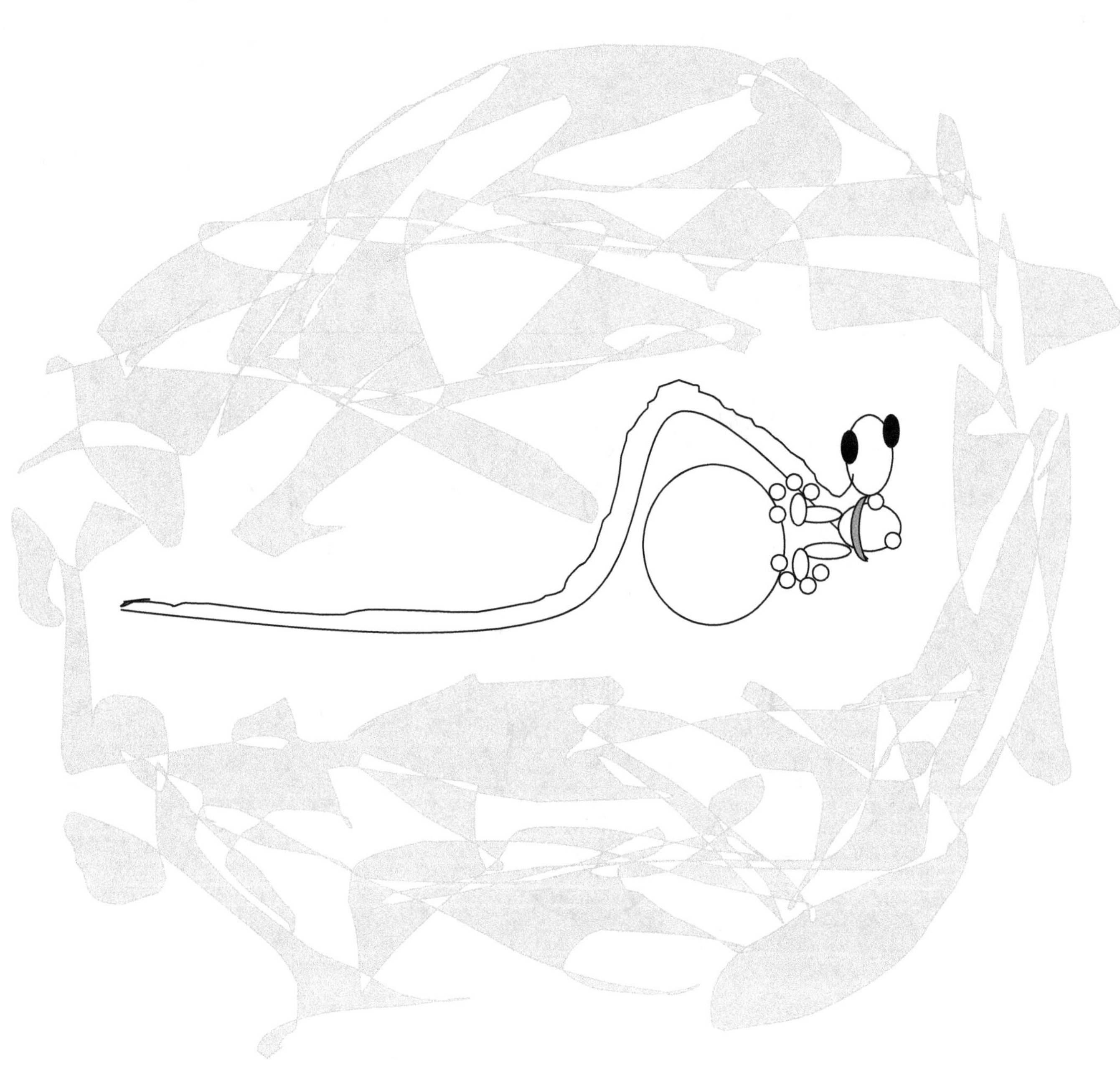

I eat food.

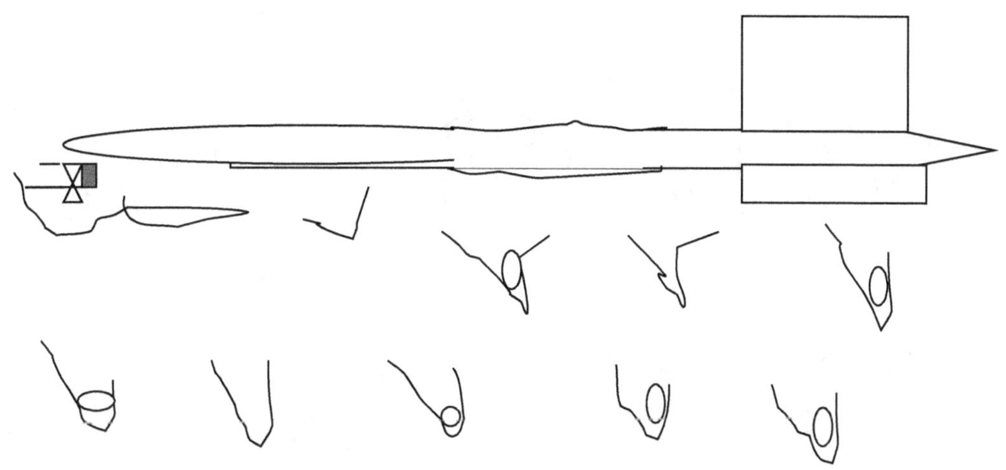

I eat food too!

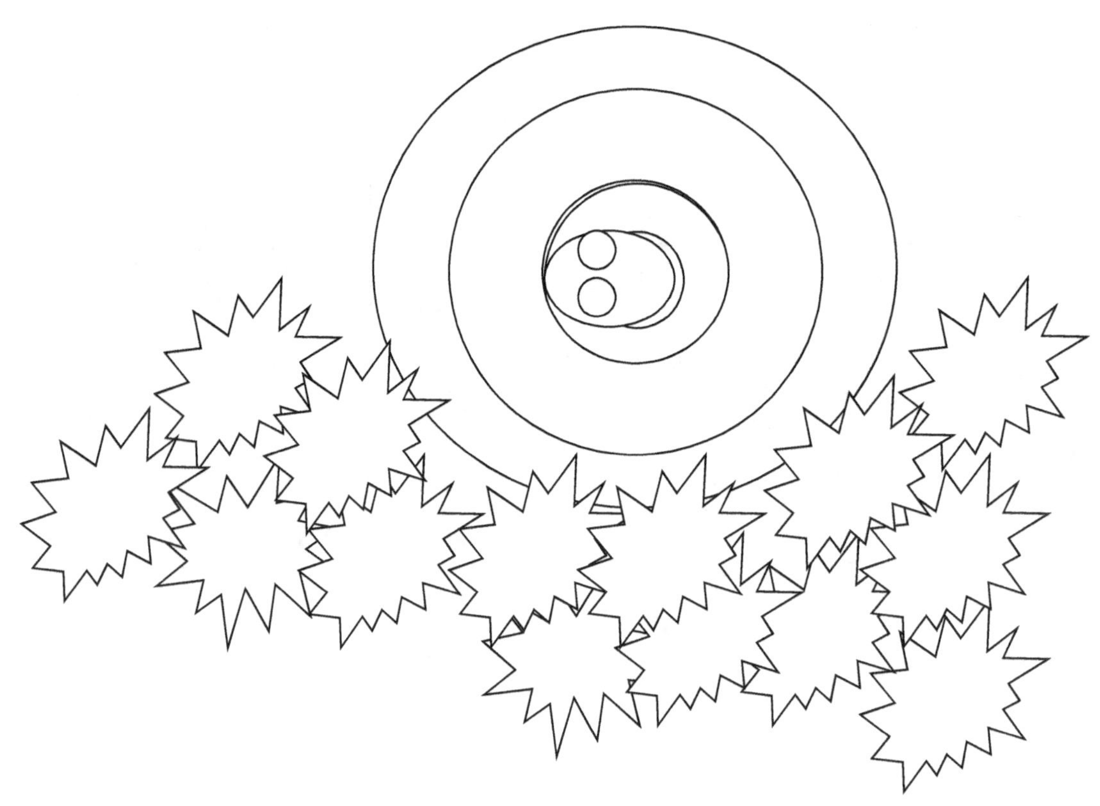

I sleep and coil up.

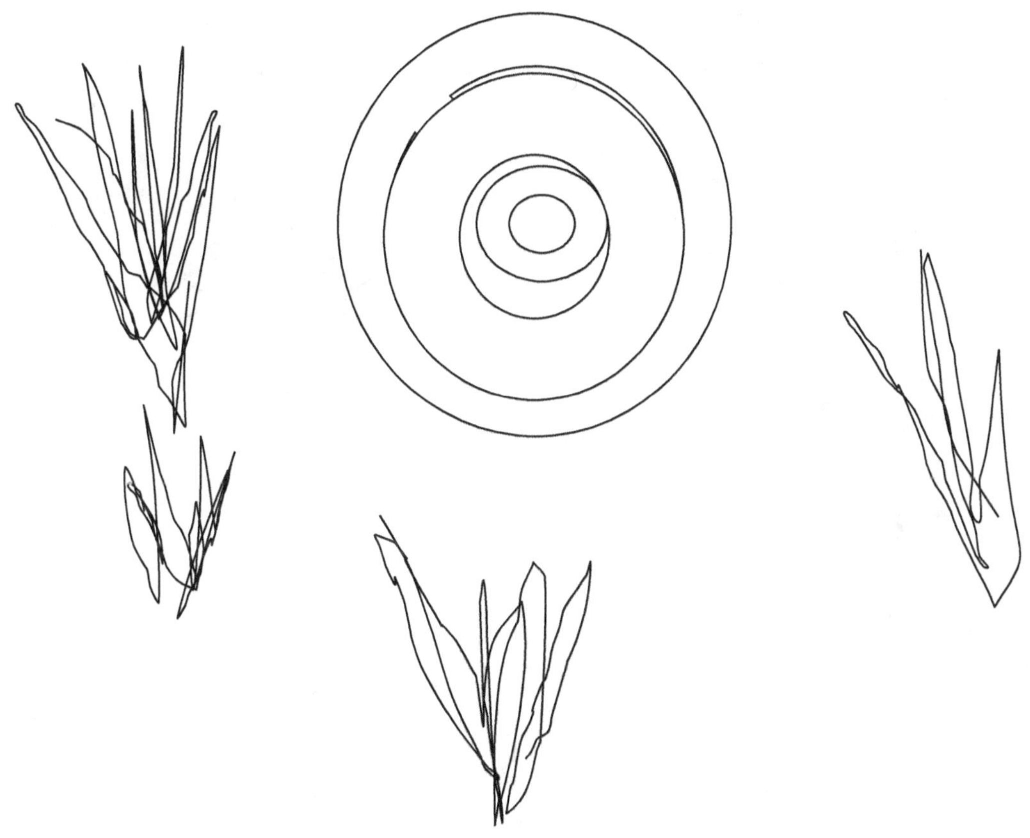

I sleep and coil up too!

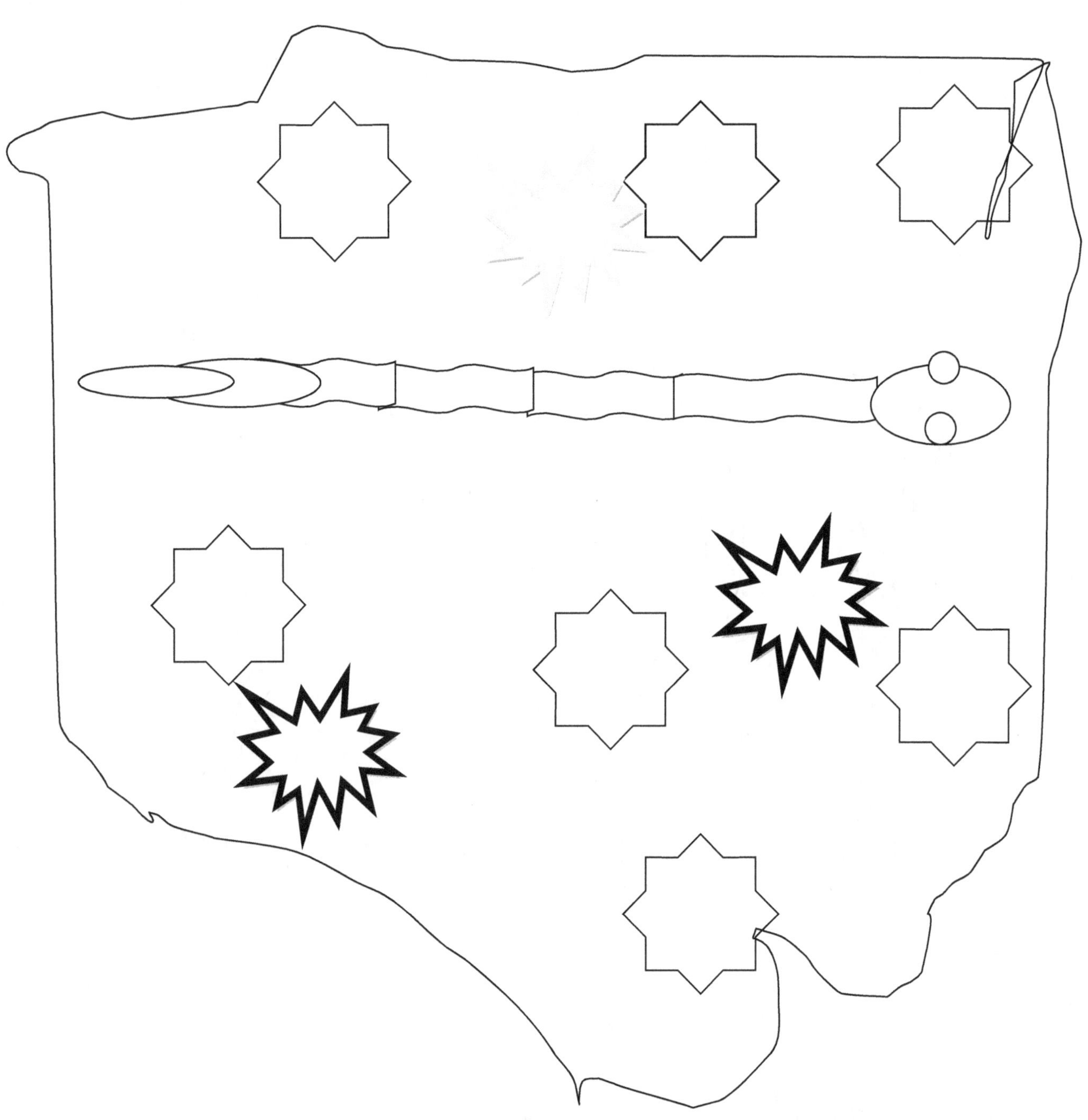

Watch me wriggle.

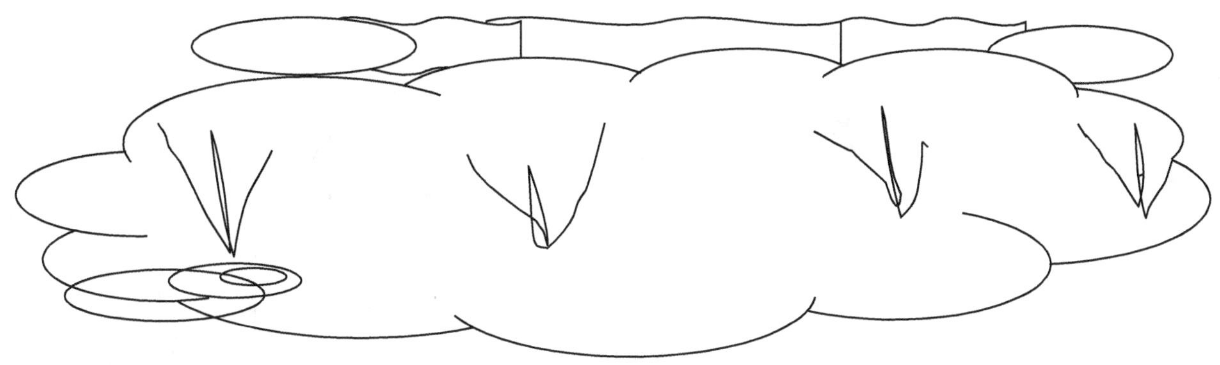

I can wriggle too!

The snake jumps from trees.

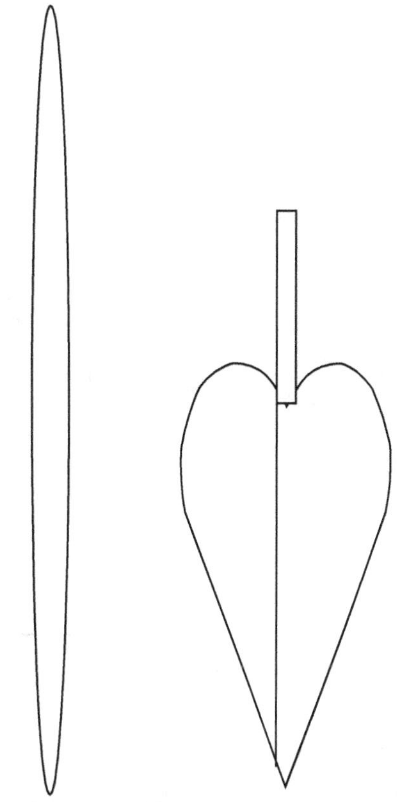

The worm jumps from leaves too!

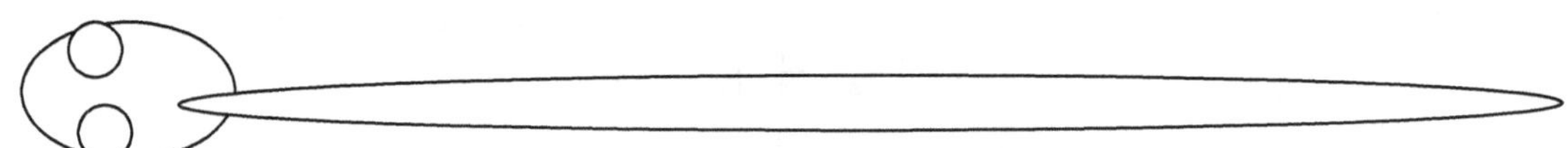

A snake is long.

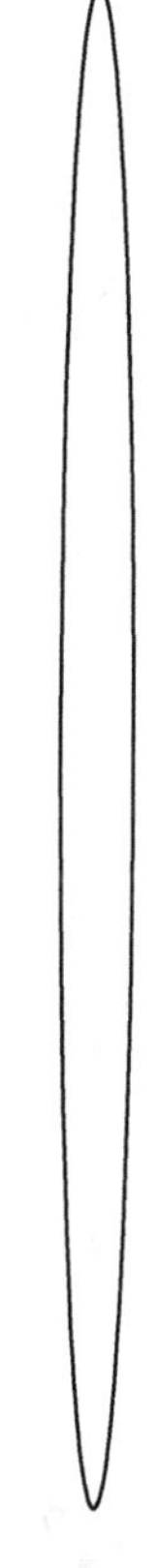

A worm is long too!

The snake enjoys the sun.

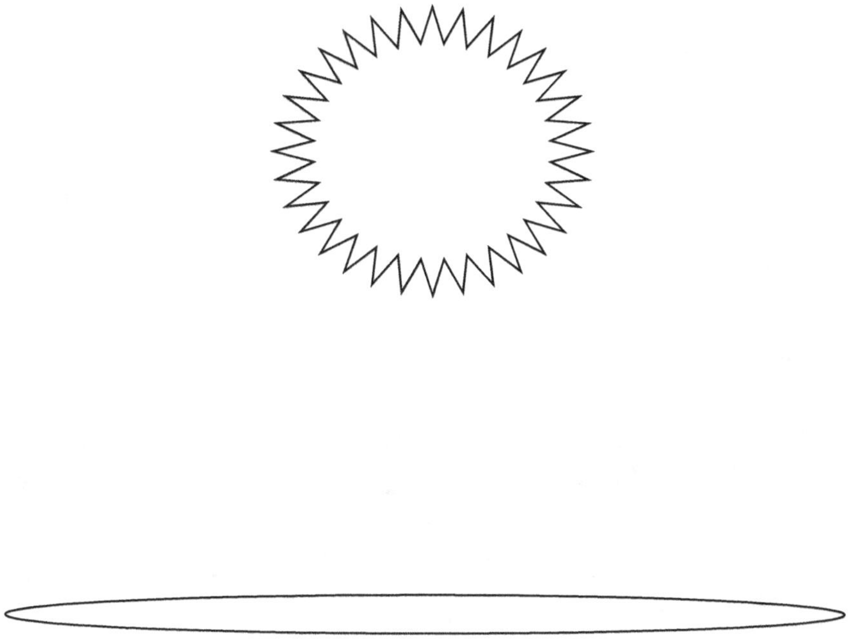

The worm enjoys the sun too!

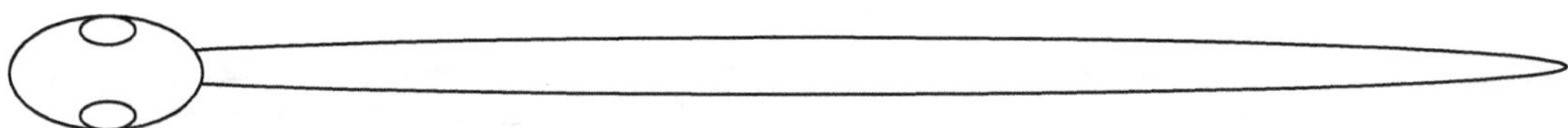

A snake has no limbs.

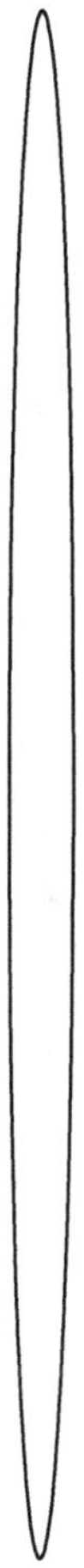

A worm has no limbs too!

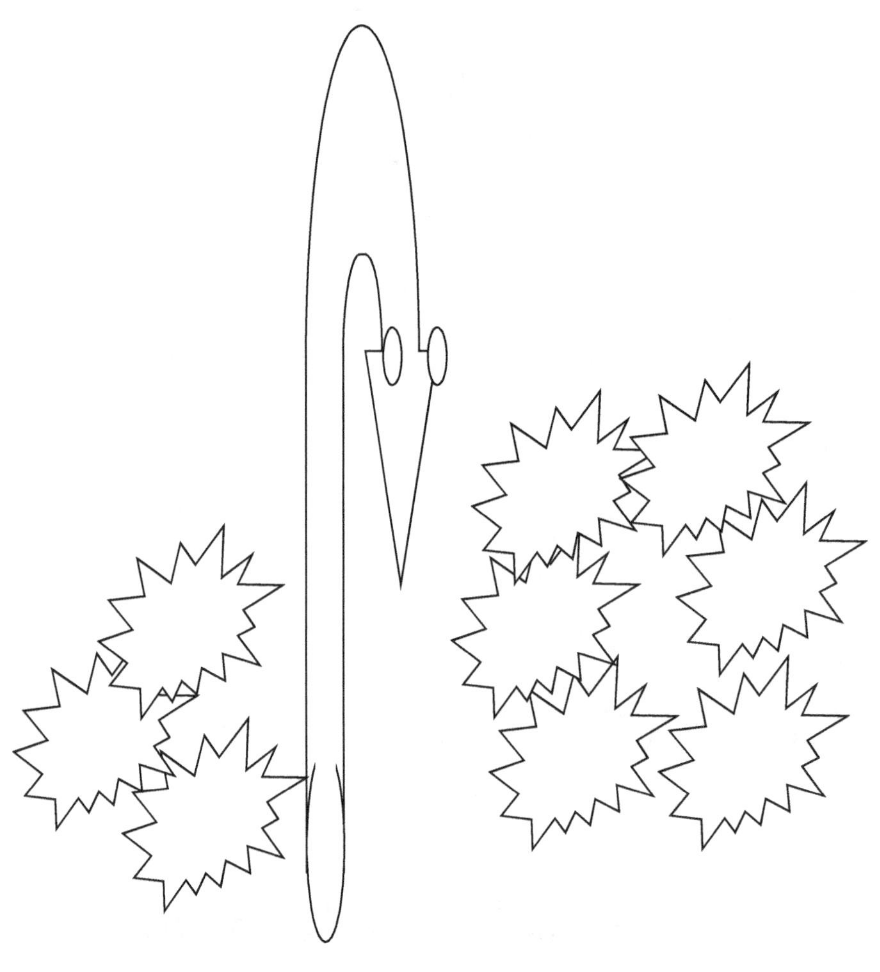

A snake loves to look for food.

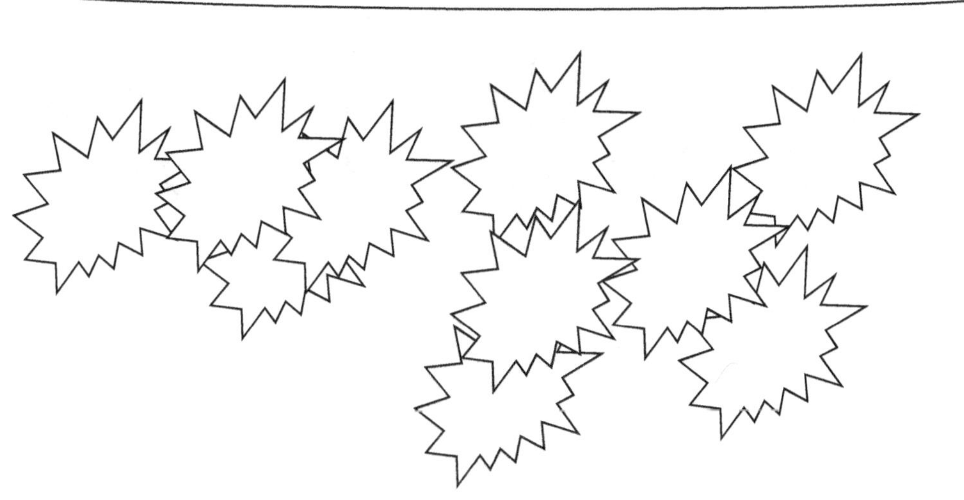

A worm loves to look for food too!

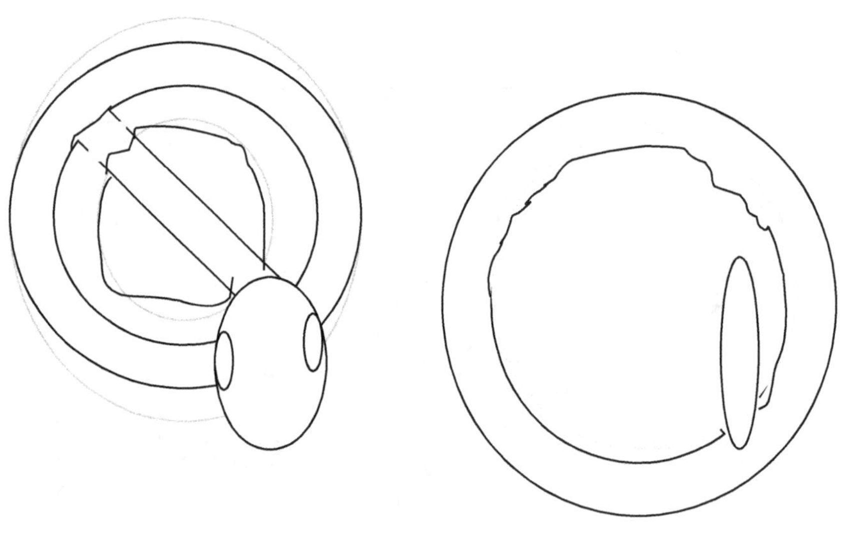

Both can make a pair!

What We Have in Common Brim Coloring Books

Crocodile and Alligator
Turtle and Tortoise
Starfish and Octopus
Worm and Snake
Vulture and Turkey
Ostrich and Emu
Weka and Kiwi
Bat and Rat
Camel and Llama
Duck and Pelican
Kangaroo and Wallaby
Pig and Tapir
Skunk and Squirrel
Hedge and Anteater
Cat and Owl
Elephant and Rhinoceros
Dog and Fox
Buffalo and Bull
Leopard and Cheetah
Horse and Zebra